SUMMER WITH THE GODS

SEVENTY-THREE POEMS

SEVENTY-THREE POEMS

SUMMER
WITH THE
GODS

WRITING ELEVEN

PETER HAGUE

Summer With The Gods

First published in 2021
by Peter Hague Concept Design Art Direction

ISBN 978-1-8382746-4-1

Cover design, layout, typography and cover art by:
Peter Hague Concept Design Art Direction.

Cover illustration from an image called:
'Discovering New Gods' by Peter Hague (e-brink)

Photographs by Peter Hague

Other photographs by Winifred Hague and Lara Newton.

www.peterhague.com

A catalogue record for this book is available
from the British Library.

SUMMER WITH THE GODS

Seventy-three poems

ALSO BY PETER HAGUE

Hope in the Heart of Hatred
Twenty-nine poems

Gain of Function
One hundred and two poems

I went unnoticed into the deadly quiet –
the labour of my words spent, yet unsaid.
They rippled, at best, in a telling quake –
a landslide of buried lines, unread.

Or was I still lost
in that original, first and muted fate?
"Go and find the Second Silence," I said.
"Fill it with words – it is not too late."

'The Second Silence' – Peter Hague

Be responsible in all your actions and condemnations

and your rights will follow.

Don't sell your soul

to gods, devils or bandwagons.

INTRODUCTION

This book of collected poems has grown in power and complexity over the last few years, becoming what might be called a defined fusion of intent – a sort of new magic that began to stray across its own borders. It grew into the natural spaces between the individual poems to create something approaching a loosely epic story of pseudo-mythology, semi-autobiography and a broad gathering of observation.

You will be hard pressed to find a work of poetry written in current times that is more inventive, creative or searching. 'Summer With The Gods' is a poet displaying a landmark development of his talent – one that will define a period of re-invention which began to take place around 2016. If you have read Peter Hague's earlier books of poetry you will already understand something about his life and work and his mission to present to the public his various writings, reaching back a good way into the previous century. This new book, however, seems a step beyond that, and an attempt to understand what it is that still drives him to write. When asked this question he will say that while editing some of his early work he began to write new poetry and it was of a quality that, once again, seemed worth pursuing. His life experiences over the previous decades had provided him with a much greater understanding of who he was and what his place in the world might be. This broadened outlook gathered a new energy to his work that had a lot of latent fuel in the tank. 'Summer With The Gods' is just a part of this gathering of words yet stands alone as a wonderful entertainment as much as anything – a poet beginning to stretch his legs and move forward. Other poems from this period and those developed from it, will emerge in due course and entertain us with their own assured light.

His previous book entitled: 'Gain of Function' was for him, a release into published freedom and contains many memorable and active poems. In fact, there are no dismissible poems in his work – all his poems have something to say and something worth saying. It will be notable in all his books that he moves very easily from moments of semi-comic banter and intrinsic humour to scathing declarations of injustice and treachery. He occasionally has things to say about the dishonest veneer of party politics and the false vision of the world as played through the eyes of the mainstream media, which he says has thick layers of bandwagon agenda smeared all over it.

It is hard to describe exactly where Peter Hague's work might fit in a general appraisal of it for instinct and influence but on his own list of poetic gods and influential poets, he rates such names as Kathleen Raine, T. S. Eliot, Emily Dickinson, Philip Larkin, Edward Thomas, Anne Sexton, Sylvia Plath and Robert Lowell. It is noticeable that those last three names are linked by the so-called 'confessional period', placed between the late 1950s to the end of the sixties and although Peter Hague was in his teens then, and not writing poetry, it is nevertheless, in looking for the roots of his work, a place we might begin to look, since the backbone of it seems to be at least in-part, driven by an intriguing autobiographical investigation; albeit developed with imagist coding. Much of this 'search', as we may call it, is based on the endless cycle of proactive yearnings for the simple truths about life and the role that reason and understanding play in our thoughts, as well as in our daily discoveries and awakenings. One thing is certain though, he manages to inject into his work a constant newness of unfailing excitement.

PETER HAGUE – WRITING ELEVEN

THE PHOTOGRAPHS

A word on the photographs: In no way are these photographs intended to directly illustrate the poems in this book, they have been attached to some poems simply because they lent a mood or a whim to the overall suggestion, similar to the way I used photographs in my first book: 'Hope in the Heart of Hatred', intending only to collect a valid atmosphere from my own past. In this latest book the pictures do a similar service, but sometimes feel more directly contrived. I decided on this strategy in order to provide the reader with small islands of relief.

All these photographs were taken by me – either at some point in the last decade or especially to enhance a moment of this book. That may sound like a contradiction to my first words on this subject, but I can assure the reader that I am generally against using imagery to enhance poems and I strongly believe that any such imagery should ultimately be the work of the reader, in their own minds. As an example I have placed a photograph adjacent to these words here, and although these paragraphs are essentially about my book: 'Summer With The Gods', there is no direct connection between the two – except, of course, in abstract details and the overall scheme of things.

VISITATIONS

RUMOURS

OBSTACLES

ENCRYPTIONS

REPRISALS

SUMMER

WITH THE

GODS

SEVENTY-THREE POEMS

PART ONE
VISITATIONS

A WATCHER-GOD

What concoctions did earth boil up
with rain, lightening and misfortune?
Mud that churned on rolling plates
so only the energy of persistence could follow.
God made notes, but did not plunge a hand
into that great chaos –
a vortex, drowning under its own control.

Instead, he became a watcher-god –
expectant of worship at every cost;
every penalty upon our servile lives –
and the daily thread of unhealed prayers
holding back a flawed humanity,
with all its inborn frailty, carefully unsaid.
It was a faith that loved, only in demonstration;
or with the displacement of a kindness;
or just sincere desperation.

It was beyond any measure of truth or beauty,
and would steal the clothes of any stranger
to acquire what its ego refused to borrow –
those missing skills of patience and empathy,
plundered to ease a world of torment
and undeniable, god-sized sorrow.

THE SECOND SILENCE

I cannot pretend I did not rail against my fate
by over-thinking far too much and far too late.
Or by allowing the suspicious energy
of negativity, pride and jealous thought
to pollute my naturally sentimental state.

I had to tell my quietest voice
to go and find the second silence –
to avoid the whispers of this treacherous world –
the languid talk that slurs its vowels
inside a barely lucid frame.

I have lived a puzzled life –
alone and aloof in a rigid tower,
where the blurring flock of a circling world
seemed one step obstinate – a turn impure.
My second life was more easily moved –
it tiptoed aside, as light as sparks –
as frivolous and redundant as breath on a chandelier,
or the cascade into silence from a brushed harp.

I went unnoticed into the deadly quiet –
the labour of my words spent, yet unsaid.
They rippled, at best, in a telling quake –
a landslide of buried lines, unread.

Or was I still lost
in that original, first and muted fate?
"Go and find the Second Silence," I said.
"Fill it with words – it is not too late."

WHERE WE LIVE

Life is a death sentence –
and that is where we live.

There is always life in the bundle of travelling –
between the sentence and the death.

And that is where we live: in the travelling.
In the shallow root of it all.

In the perfection of uncertain balance.
In the adventure of the spanning bridge.

Arrival is feared, though somewhat welcome –
accepted as huge, unkind, unavoidably certain.

And that is where we live.

I FORGOT TO LOOK AT THE SKY

1
I got out of bed when the world was still grey;
a murmur of colour spawned in its east.
I looked with borrowed, poets' eyes,
and scribbled something down to cast it from my head.
I did not look at the sky again – I returned to bed.

I am wondering now what the weather might be?
And what details of it I might have gleaned
had I looked at the sky in a normal way.

When I rise again, it will be without poets' eyes –
more likely with the eyes of ordinary men;
eyes that need to know
what sort of day is going to break –
not just ponder in subtle raptures
over a romantic, easterly glow.
It will be a day in which to get things done
and I will require fair weather on that ancient road –
the road to celebrity is oversold,
yet apparently the only way to get ahead –
the most we can expect to win.
But the label of 'poet' is hard to define
and should never be discussed

among the listenings of living men.
And certainly not placed above talk of weather,
or in passing comments about general health.

It is up to others to declare a poet –
either living, almost alive or famously dead.

2
That evening, I saw a hopeful laureate –
being at best, a celebrity, on game show tv.
He quietly introduced himself as a living poet.
And even though others had crowned his verse,
it still seemed a somewhat presumptuous title –
since he may still only represent to them
(those idling king-makers of dubious intent)
a mild infatuation in the theatre of pretence.
A rattler of other mens' bones.

It is wise to take counsel on stages such as these –
he should have admitted his celebrity first:
as one who had attempted to write his heart
in a way that was hopefully not quite the worst.
That would have been more accurate, I think,
than a living poet vouching for himself –

a 'celebrity poet' and subscribed academic
appearing as a book you would not rush to open,
while leading a team to the questionable goal
of increased celebrity, at the very height.
But at least the team might provide some knowledge
to pass through this captain's starry head.
Or lend him some of their unused matches
for the striking clichés lighting his shed.

I do not think you can be a game show poet.
The best you can offer is to know the names
of those whom others had already crowned,
and in similar, fanciful ways.

For no one is a poet these days.

The world has got its sizes wrong
and is too broadly influenced by sawn-off news –
their putrefying comics and literary magazines
are full of pictures now – and words, now and again.
It is a random marketing of dying flowers
that pave the way for honest men,
who look to the sky for knowledge of weather,
having no need of a laureate's pen.

THE RUBBER LIVES OF ASTRONAUTS

I have grown a new belief – rooted stronger
than faith or church – nurtured
within my brambled heart for sixty years.
Not new or dangerous, unless you are a god
and tired of the trick of infinite time –
or have frowned enough at the warp and weft
of the unreliable cosmic clock.
It is a belief that does not require
the dubious tools of age-old gods.
It was passed as a seed at my rigorous birth
and I have watered it like a nuisance ever since –
sometimes with urine, sometimes with tears,
and with the churning waves of stirring years.

It is a doorway I have stood in, week by week,
tapping in the code of freedom, in good faith.
Now it opens – an eager flower –
with the explosive petals of a pampered bud.
Its emerging light falls on my step and at my feet –
a swirling energy – a living thing –
rocket-fuelled with fossils from an earth of trees.

None of these natural forces can survive
without our designs, made of rubber and dreams –

the vibrating days – the flexible wheels
and the smudging of hard lines.
We are an unstoppable, oscillating human growth,
where all life is fungal-like and equipped with spores.
We blow into the ways where we can latch our hope,
with a shower of semen or the dust from our skin –
or the thunderous power of a rocket's claws.
We are a very substantial living thing.
We can pollute and spoil,
yet wield the magic of temporary gods.

We will finally convert these gifts of nature
into the shapes of spaceships, grown in soil.
We will set out, then, on that baffling ocean
of galaxies, stardust and devotional toil.
Unfolding leaves will become our sails
for the gentle power of solar wind,
as we are pushed by the prayers
of an endless summer
into an infinite universe of glorious suns.

MISSION: AND BEYOND

My solitude is manifest in a cold corner of the Moon.
I am limp in a crater; abandoned in black and white –
weak and tight amongst the seminal debris
of a rain of stone. The horizon seems too close here
and space appears more dangerous than on Earth.
It is bigger and more valuable – uncomfortable too,
where the mood of infinity
calms the rattle of local chaos.

It is an immense cave –
a stacked warehouse, full of stars,
and me, a dim workman on the loneliest night shift,
looking for orders to assemble and despatch.
Playing that ignorant game of efficiency,
with its worn rubber-stamp.
We are allowed to forget the other, tormenting present,
even if we still harbour a nightmare past.
But for all my authority with wires and beams,
I cannot play them far enough
to span the common sense
of this boundless brain of space.

I feel more alone here with each silence –
as empty as Lee Harvey Oswald

in the Schoolbook Depository –
down in the restroom, drinking Coke –
trying to look natural – as someone shot the President –
as if he ever could look natural, with a face like his –
a face of chosen guilt.
He was conscripted by suspicion itself
to look through the square window of his alibi;
to wait for the police to bestow brief innocence
upon his now famously awkward head.

Just as I look now – peering through a culpable visor,
that hides the truth for we suspected assassins –
anticipating a light debriefing on a treacherous Earth,
that has already shunned our re-entry to life.

For Oswald was not a natural man,
as I am unnatural here,
in the dry Dallas, Texas of the Moon.
No one knows if I shot out the sun,
or claimed this shadowed crater for its creeping cold,
but I will be blamed anyway if the mission fails –
"I am a patsy."

Mission Control are drinking beer and champagne

and celebrating a victory which is all their own –
happy their precocious rocket worked at all,
with its overrated technology of tin cans and fire.
I have lost everything by coming here.
I have lost my way. I have lost my keys.
Though I may have found the meaning of austere.
I am losing my faculties too –

I am a shivering loon on a derelict moon
in a spacesuit sealed with glue.

My memories have leaked past this polymer skin
and filled a virgin planet with their unique plague –
making an atmosphere of suppressed guilt
or at least something irresponsible and vague.
And although it may seem to register
as weak, or vacuous, or impossible to measure,
I can barely get my breath above this pressure.
I cannot see a single thing in a suddenly laden air –
it is a fog to me and weighs me down,
tired as Ophelia, beneath a watery film –
almost clear, but undeniably there.

I have tried my best, as we all must.
I have tried to swim in this dry dust.
I have attempted to photograph my presence here,
out on this unforgiving, bony limb.
I have tried to crack my helmet
and make my mind go dim.

In light of this, I have decided to explore
the value of my own existence –
a gross deviation from the scientific mission,
but the Moon is not the stone on which
this corporate adventure shall be written.
Earth's guidelines seem so rigid and futile here –
a plan, emphatically briefed, but never discussed.
In truth, it was little more than a rude intention
to take some snapshots and collect some dust.

I am going to push off this planet now
with the easy gravity of my new frogs' legs.
I am defying my superiors and going on –
to search for the remains of God instead.

I SAW THE WIND

I saw the wind this time. I saw its frowning face:
a beast, annoyed at the freedom of the promenade.
It threw our hair across our smiles –
sticking to your lipstick – outwitting my grace.
It pulled at the shirts of unflinching men,
rippling the fabric of cloth and brow.
And also the skin of short-sleeved women,
who had seemed as firm as adolescence till now.

It was a staring wind –
no match for gusty talk or blustering cities,
but one that caught the senses with its small tirade.
A mild wind, really – more an ambition;
a common grumble on the lips of God
while the sun sparked through his special cloud.

It was nothing to interest a restless kite;
a castle of sand; a disturbed crow.
Nor the ruffled gull that blinked and stood it out.
It was just something to dwell upon –
apart from a rare, seductive peace,
which was blown away now, gone.

WHY DISTANT SHIPS MOVE SO SLOW

Walking around my house at night,
with little light, except moon-smeared shadows,
I move as slowly as a distant boat –
every moment, still and measured, yet afloat...
slightly adrift perhaps and beyond control,
and far-off the sanity of a harbour wall.

I have a ponderous helm that lives in delay,
an amorphous armchair – casual in all directions.
There are safe moorings here and there
and I will loop their bollards soon enough.
First, I must interpret the sway
of my rudder's lingering, autonomous hand –
it hangs above a deep and moving tide of sand,
reaching down into this ocean soup of night.

I must also read the light and shadows
thrown upon the clouded staircase walls;
they are my constellations to steer by –
they are my oceanic charts – sextant and all.
They are cast in the slant of casement windows
and strung with simple sticks and glass,
surging on the rising-tide of turning stairs
that coil the mast.

With these rigid sails and their rise and fall,
I am becalmed in a moonlit silhouette –
and set against the night's dark lamp,
with its twitching ropes and clanking bells –
the ghostly calls of far-off, restless buoys.

There is also noise from the farthest room,
the rumblings and flashings of a distant storm,
and that is where the lighthouse turns,
searching with a sudden, uncatchable dawn.
It warns of the hazards of walls and shores,
and the creaking tides of wooden floors,
and of old portraits in gilded frames:
washed from centuries of abandoned doors.

These do not concern my current voyage,
but present their subject as a formal duty –
just as I mention them now, in passing,
and purely as a measure of illustrated fixity:
for they are sometimes tellingly adorned
with the collected labours of a staged profession –
pertinent clothes and emblematic toys,
such as Captain Thorpe, here, pictured in uniform,
with a folded spyglass for assured authority.

He takes note of the weather, out in the offing,
which is inline with the integrity of the picture rail –
this, his varnished stretch of beached antiquity
gathering the dust of recent tides –
drying out the vapours of his living oil.

My own ship is predicted within this telling frame –
very far out and moving slow.
Making headway against the boisterous swell,
with still an ocean's expanse to go.
But while I am master of these swelling tides
I will steer a course for our stranded love.
It will take me past our breathing bed,
where you sleep fast, with your lovely head
and offer no prayers for my safe return.

BRINGING NEW ENERGY TO THE SAME DEATH

Is that me, rolling in from the distant offing?
An undulation on that great plain we call the sea.
I am an energy, begun in reverberation –
a stirring eye of wind across a cold, unstable soup.
A passion – swelling – where life's procession
begins to shape our face and sense of reason,
as might an artist's thumbs in a slip of clay.

My future is a beach somewhere, some far-off day,
and I will warn its keepers of my eventual coming –
signalling with flailing limbs and harmless rumour,
and with the dark sticks of tidal drumming –
a rhythm telling the confirmation
and the full intention of my final hour.

This semaphore of arms and minutes
will multiply the rolling years,
until the day I break on evening's limits –
a windmill with smashed and battered sails;
a dissipating energy that leaves for God;
a cautious hiss, inflating prayers and spaces;
a litany of grief, either echoed or completed
by the chaliced mouths of hopeful voices.

They say nothing of themselves,
but raise a smiling glass as I pass their hearts.

I will study old details of ritual chores,
to be assembled with pebbles and dead-crabs' claws.
These remnants will chart the viability of horizons
and shape the destiny of all who follow:
those yet to claim their personal path
through the robot mills of unstitching-entropy,
which is all there is – though said poetically,
and with a last rush of foaming breath.

THE HUNTING WAVES

Be careful of the sea,
it is pitiless some days – a hunter.
It will see you fooling on the edge of land
and wash you free of joy and life.
You will become an entombed beast
from ancient times,
surprised in mud for millions of years...

Unless they fish you out tonight,
beleaguered by death and limp of mind –
not quite the you, you wanted left behind –
bedraggled and stilled by life's adventure.
A torch in your face
and the sea... sneaking back
to its brutal gloom.

AFTERMATH

I was watching, that disturbing night –
after the storm had knocked itself out
and left a blackness all about.
The tide drew back in diminishing rows –
breaking in lines of thinning waves
that seemed to be holding hands,
while short of breath –
a performance to the brink of death?
They bowed as actors, leaving the stage –
stepping back with creeping shoes,
into a darkness flanked by theatre wings,
no longer lit by the sleeping town.
It was a darkness I did not want to know.
Nor did I want to hear its sound:
a low voice of hissing death,
that slid, gurgling off the edge of land.
I saw the illusive stars of ghostly buoys;
they were cast far out, as winking eyes –
the pilots of that shut-down night,
with rusty bells that yearned for home.
Then I knew the storm and all its magic,
had left a spark of deeper light:
a wound, signalling to every nation
beyond the dark edge of our tidal blood.

CIVILISATION OF THE DAMNED
Scientific Highs and Lows

There is a world now
beyond natural weed,
done with science
to fuck you up.
It lasts like silence
in comatose dreams
until your parents come
to switch you off.

WHEN I AM DEAD I WILL BE WIND

When I am dead I want to blow as the wind blows.
Not in the new places – or looking for Cathy,
on some high desolation of frozen rocks.
I want to blow through our old rooms,
hosting days now lost
to the cruelty of ruthless history.

I would be a wind, set fair to watch the past;
a light breeze of astonishing air.
I would rattle windows and open doors –
a permissible-cooling-familiar-draught.

Or I will brush across your skin sometimes
and make you laugh.

LEAKS IN THE RUSE

1

Would it be so difficult for these treacherous days
to ever speak back to my whittling heart?
To proclaim the intention of universal law,
or at least something vague, made transparent and pure?
Something belonging to synchronicity, or fate,
a guide to a foundational pause for thought –
a regular quest for the understanding of our place,
gathered through the observation of the willing extant.
Perhaps an obsequious quiet of conducted discipline,
as within the structured reverence of a worthy science?
Maybe a ritual, assigned only to a portion of each hour –
offered to the proponents of mysterianism?

2

Here in suburbia, I question these unremitting days,
sitting calendar-like in God's awful choir.
Waiting for tomorrow's inevitable chime
to pipe-up with duty and the clockwork of chores.
Or the blocking hypocrisy of frustration and delays
and the half-full philosophy of half-open doors.
Irritation is lounging within a ruptured peace,
tinkering amongst the houses and the washing lines.
And the wild clods of garbage cans, half unseen,

where hails the plastic portent of peeling paint.

The nature of days never looks back,
as it unfolds its entropically-centred plan.
Pretending to dismiss our myth of minutes,
which we invented in a moment of genuine faith –
something to keep track of our brave adventures
as we strike into the seam of its destructive coal.
Time can only be built upon with diligent sense,
and the pure fuel of an acceptable goal.

The nature of days is rigid and unforgiving,
especially when hosting suburbia, as they do.
In that brilliant, blatant, nonchalant way –
and with a slight veil of cultivated woe.
Its machinery ensures all the accents are right,
and the various placements are accurate and exact.
Positioned off-centre and with variable colours
to smear illusion into the valuable mix.

There is always an eye for random discrepancy,
such as broken arms and bruised legs.
Or those minor fidgets and their flailing limbs –

and perhaps the unexpected turning of a head?
And it is heard in the imperfection of rolling wheels,
with tyres, hissing-loose their patient breath.
Yes, there are leaks in the fabric of this fond deception
and they are intentional, I guess –
a concocted valve for the pressure of truth.

3
But there are just too many arguments going on
and clamorous scenes at neighbours' doors.
Too many bird squabbles on the high, guttered slates;
just too much fuss for one gathering of claws.
There is also the endless, scuffing trail
of the movement of polished or blistered shoes –
those impressionist footsteps that paint their mission
with the syncopated slapping of driven feet.

Cars slip by under the stealth of transmission,
smoothed into travel by a hierarchy of gears,
and the occasional bus of grinding humans –
the indifferent cogs of unsaid years.
All this seems adequate on the sunniest days,
with me, bemused amid a garden of toil.
Poised in a world that would be pleasantly diminished,

if the days were not so lavish with detail –
and my own mind not so flavoured by it all.
Not so deeply fathomed by the fancies of clouds,
that sleep their shadows over smiling lawns,
repeating in the quiet glide of window panes,
where reflections slide in to heal the calm.

4

I turn my music off to listen – not just for rumours,
but for the science of clues – I also listen for pauses now,
and not just those stiffening in a clock of mirrors –
nor in the windless repose of un-minding trees.

I listen for the tell-tale leaks in the ruse –
hiding in the loose, netted fabric of the weave.
Those betraying moments that are whispered aloud,
where you hear an unkind god, laughing up his sleeve,
or see a giant eyeball peering from a cloud.

PART TWO
RUMOURS

THE NATURAL VOICE

A silent heart will find a way to speak.
Humans are ingenious listeners;
they will find a channel,
or tie a string between two cans.
Or there will be sound waves from an offering soul
that we can tune in with a simple tweak.

We built the dish-like giant ears
to listen to the cloth of a crumpled sky.
It could not be ironed out by theory or physics,
or imagined in the soul, or the head, or the eye.

It is our nature to listen to a natural voice
that comes from the heart, or comes from the air –
and exists beyond the shallows of company,
and where our outermost senses listen and listen.
And where they lean into the darkness
to rummage deep.

THE IMPORTANCE OF CLOUDS

I could attempt to disperse the clouds
but clouds do not listen to lesser gods –
self-proclaimed gods, who rule by chaos –
yet prove weak and powerless
when countering the manifestations of clouds.
To transient clouds we are conceited meddlers –
scribbling fools seeking majesty in poems.
Or some other improvisation of impatient thought
that turns our rutted cogs a measure.
Clouds do not move aside for poetry,
they are the scenery of its highest domain –
shifting or still – glorious or dark –
without clouds, we would not have found
our breath of words –
these fleeting animations we must name at once,
using reflexes forged in the hearts of the ancients.
It is an aura of sound without formal structure;
a synthesis of moods, seething in rapture;
a momentary recognition of glimpsed potential,
lending brief clues and mysterious epithets
to the vague identity of fleeting gods.

And that is where poetry ignites into song –
with playful clouds full of words and faces.

All looking back with liquid stirrings,
        then gone.

The blue sky and sun are intruders in this
and have never been part of poetry at all.
They are a skulking happiness, hidden in vagary;
a deluded world we cannot connect with;
a lingering place where all time waivers
and the parched dictionary slams its words shut.
It is an iron mouth in futile meditation;
a proven stage for the thinking of nothing;
a distraction of belongings and soothing heat.
It rubs its lotions of desire and silence
into the accepting canvas of our translucent skin.
This is the silence of sun and beauty –
an easy page, neither turned from, nor begun –
the host of paradise in one long sigh,
parching our living entity into a husk.

The sun and the sky are a lasting covenant,
hiding behind the cloudy words of night –
when the smoke moves aside for the poetry of stars,
revealing the eloquence of our darker terrors.

A RETREAT INTO BOOKS

One morning, your eyes became a poem
and slipped inside a late anthology
of the confessional poets, published in 1969.
Your eyes were seeking something vital –
something not found in their own heart, or mine;
some missing value, where we became a silence
that turned as a page and set us apart.

Years later, that book is still on my shelf.
It is a union of the dead, waiting us out –
bearing the transfigured spirit of determined eyes,
smoothed in the courage of eager prayer.
Each prayer is confessed into a page of sacrifice –
where the blesséd reverie of your silenced book,
hosts a telling spread of the inkblot test –
where we splattered ink between a soothing fold.

It settled all rumour into convenient science.
It convenes in your absence and settles all doubt,
while not fearing for the sanity of contemporary words,
so rhythmically garbled in a slashing of lines.
Nor in the abbreviated slaughter of stranded quotes –
those hasty volleys of sanctioned deceit.

But this, your chosen book, is precious to me.
I open it occasionally – a welcome door.
I step inside the vault of your sleeping heart,
or the opening rose of that missing thought,
where your poem-eyes settled into beguiling shapes
that became lip-like sirens – pooling with flowers.

In this secret place of silence and grace
we will meet again and talk for hours.

DEPRESSION'S EMBRACE

I feel safe in the nest of my partizan house,
surrounded by walls of depression and books.
It is as good a house as any – as good as it gets.
I feel welcome, as long as I remain quiet;
not tempted to scream by the cuckoo of stress –
that moment we lean too far and fall away,
into the disconnection of trust.

Depression becomes overwhelming there.
We hang on to a senseless soul we can barely feel;
a hand in a turmoil of water and oil –
and that is 'she' – our depression; our rain; our soil.
We can plant something good here and watch it grow.
She is the flower of pain, appearing in person;
a germination beyond which, nothing is certain.

We have to stay within the blue of ourselves
and live in that summered colour for a while.
We cannot row back if we let it go –
the walls will collapse without our foraging brains
      and it is true –
our depression needs to know –
every bright detail we ourselves contain.

You and your doubt support each other,
as enduring scales, weighing invaluable odds.
It is a loose embrace – a sealed tomb –
a defused bomb – the safety of the womb.
Depression need not kill you though, so hold on.

Depression can be a creative force –
an inspiration from a darker source.
Sometimes depression will glow as a lamp,
shining in the fullness of all you fear –
but she is the true spirit of Lazarus –
the divine resolution – the transcending dark horse.
Stay mounted and you can ride her clear.

ANOTHER KIND OF HAT

I have bought a hat to wrap around my casual thoughts.
Something to wear when I walk my cautious mind –
stepping through the high-wire streets
where I cannot tread
without the tripwire-maze of boobytrapped shoes.
I go high above the wrecks and the potholes,
to where a kind of 'nodded' passage thrives.
It is a channel for cargo – damaged – confused.
A gentler path where confidence survives.

Our sanity of clay is slammed onto a potters' wheel –
and with one slip we are slightly toppling.
We oscillate with the uncertainty of the unreal,
where the un-smothered body leaves our trust exposed.
There are too many surfaces of uncomfortable fear –
I long for my bed, my chair, my repose.
And I have angled my hat in a jaunty way,
to contradict the uncertain oscillation I feel.

I bought an overcoat to match my hat
and became an instant parody then,
of something – anything – of this or that –
some pompous twat in a Homburg hat?

Now I must wear a scarf and gloves
to negate the pretensions of all of the above.
Let us call it a 'winter device',
and claim that cleverly subtle ploy.
Let us limp with the lame excuse of cold weather –
no longer an ikon of fashion or wisdom –
not at all free and barely a boy.

LET US NOT CARE AND BE SCANDALOUS

1

When I returned to the studio after lunch
my boss stopped me on the way through the door.
He was chatty and full of retail advice;
insistent on telling me where he spent his gold.
He was no doubt certain, in his superior way,
that I was servile enough,
during the tensions of shopping,
to have been misled, while fancifully pondering
the merest of cheap rewards.

But I was happy with the paperback I had rescued,
and was reverberating with the poems of Paul Verlaine.
Yet I listened to my boss anyway,
since he blocked my path and ruled the town.
He was one of those who sought to simplify,
with his shallow mind and his universal ways.
He was an egotistical exponent of self-truth –
one proclamation and three steps short
of the meddling onslaught of Arthur Rimbaud.
And to some extent, he too was an ebullient youth,
even as an artistic businessman in middle-age –
a man still in love with his noble hair.

I eventually thanked him for his foisted guidance
and returned to my easel to paint the sky.

I often painted the sky in the afternoon;
it was the therapeutic part of my lenient job.
My skies were confident and gloriously proud,
and usually blue with a harmless light.
They became a periphery of inoffensive cloud
that was always animated and billowing shy –
all the time happy, in their ponderous mischief,
to be moving carefully out of sight.

I was good at capturing that charming mood
of slow, derivative, rolling currents –
though I sometimes painted with a clear blue wash,
so the eye would search, to breathe that lovely air,
finding it there, in the relief of looking.
It was all dependent on scale and voracity,
and the necessary breath for an emotional scene.
And the invisible quota of required hope,
gauged to entertain a fulfilling mood.

All this was before offering the certainty of deliverance;
and there was always a quantity of electricity involved.
The poster and viewer would meet themselves sparking,
on a beach of sand in the best flush of weather –
the contagious glow, tapped from my angle-poise lamp,
which shone as summer throughout the year.

My posters were like happy ships –
they sailed off on winter nights.
Their sails, of course, were billowing clouds,
set to exult the expectations of veneer.

2
I understand my boss had been trying to help,
suggesting places where I might save money.
For it was money paid by him, and which I suspect
he still regarded as wealth of his own –
at least until the ink wore off the paper notes
or an ancient contractual blood-rite expired.
He advised me to buy a house I could ill-afford –
"An investment," he said. "A legacy for the future."
I would later thank him for that long-term vision
and for some other prudent advice he offered.

I suppose to some extent, my life was his
and I did not question that apparent law.
I was his apprentice and neophyte –
a journeyman, an understudy – his encore?
He taught me everything I know and tried for more,
which has served me well – beyond complaint,
though there were wild and personal things
I did not understand or want, and as such,
were mine to carefully ignore.

My knowledge of poetry was self-infused;
my boss was only interested in the suspicions therein:
the philandering ways of lauded poets –
the rumour, gossip and the transactions of sin.
The tediums of morality, left languishing in the gutter
or in the amorous fields of beds and blessings.
These were the only worthwhile seductions for him,
he did not elaborate on the contortions of words,
denouncing them as nothing more
than ungrateful explanation.

3

Forty years on, my boss is dead –
struck by lightening a decade ago.

I live in a big house now which, even in death,
he still considers to be his own.
Or so it plays out in my paranoid mind
and to some extent, I agree, of course –
there was never doubt, or fairness of choice –
he being my mentor and Master of the World.

Yet I still have my book of Verlaine's poems,
with a bus ticket marking the page I last read.
The ticket is date-stamped and turning brown,
rolling inward with an autumn edge –
an origami version of an inherited crown.

My bus-ride home that ancient night
had taken me past those same old shops
where my boss, contorting into a messiah of thrift,
had recommended their fidelity earlier in the day.
It was then I saved my place with the ticket,
that still marks the half-ungrateful hour,
where I was forced to look – partly out of respect –
and for the devilment of due contemplation at least –
as one by one these emporiums flickered shut
and have all since passed away.

4

As my life stands now, I have decided to explore –
it is never too late to pretend to exist.
I have removed the ticket and begun to read on
and I am having an affair with my boss's widow.
I live in his old mansion on the town hill,
which is worth more of his money every day.
Clytemnestra heals her romance through me
and wishes he had read more poetry to her.
Perhaps right there in the four-poster bed,
that has long since run-aground in a padded boudoir –
its lazy rocks, still treacherous and wanting
and her siren lips, still versed in enchantment.

Clytemnestra is thirteen years older than me
and there are rumours,
whispered in the billowing clouds,
or echoed in the snipes of the printing trade,
that now declare me her 'poster boy' –
or said out loud:

  "Aegisthus – The Slayer of Agamemnon".

For that is truly how we were named.

And who cares about his 'uncertain' death?
He was as ruthless as Clytemnestra anyway –
and should not have sacrificed
their daughter to the wind.

And who would have guessed that in painting the sky
with the charged meanderings of billowing clouds,
I would gain the ability to spark electrical storms,
by petitioning the gods for the merest of powers?

And I have taken to writing poetry myself,
just to prove I am almost an emancipated man;
without the annoyance of a dictating tether –
though Agamemnon's tears still water my town,
weighing their petals on sorrowful shoulders.

I also write by way of explanation
for my outlandish conduct in recent years:
leaning on the weakening gates of a fanciful Elysium
and dishonouring the role of one favoured by gods.
But for now, as the tired poet, Verlaine declared –
his heart almost over and lost in an affair:
"Let us walk forward and meet ourselves smiling:
Let us be scandalous and not care."

Verlaine
Selected Poems
Translated with an Introduction
by Joanna Richardson
Verlaine   Selected Poe

THE INJUSTICE

If injustice
is what you are striving for,
current conditions
are perfect.

PURITY OF SPIRIT

Why wait for temptation to offer payment?
You know, behind its facade is the Devil's seal;
a wax not easily broken – not even real.

There are richer complexities to undertake
that we will not have to answer for in grateful death.
They can be paid-for in kind – and in good spirit,
and keep our souls safe to draw the next breath.

BIRTH IS KING

The world seems a monstrous place –
a place of evil and abused logic.
Here, they say that death is king,
but birth is king and death is nothing.

Death cannot equal birth's endless spasms
that wrap our wounds in a healing clay.
They smear the frame of human bones
with an elaborate resistance – death sent away.

But soon, this borrowed throne of birth
will overflow and tip the balance.
And the bones of humanity will be laid bare.
Stripped of their immunity of safe deliverance.

Then the dark lord of death will reign once more –
the dark lord of death, being the nature of balance,
and the balance of nature, being a god,
above kings.

A FANTASY OF THE HUMAN RACE

We all want to live somewhere else –
somewhere not far from the anchor of birth.
Just well away from death and our human self...
and on a planet not called Earth.

A FORM OF TRUTH THROUGH PAIN

Torturers' mouths are different to ours –
they say what they like
through the misery of others.

PENANCE

And all the secretaries of the world
slept with their boss.
They could not find another saviour
who offered full employment.
It was all talk with God –
and no cigarette after.

AS THE OLD DAY FADES – WALK INTO THE NEW

We must trust our shoes from long ago.
Our shoes from the last great escape.
They walked away from anything
that did not seem content or right –
as cattle, sniffing the wind might.
Our shoes are happy and vain
and have remained so, quite unchanged
for thousands of unfettered years –
look at their proud leather heads held high.
They are a delight, if somewhat deranged.

This is the wrapping of success and age –
it coats itself in forgotten courage –
in mythologies of heroic scenes and of simple gains,
that influence the vague plan of reliable solutions.
You can try for freedom at the best of times
and also on the worst of days –
those days that bristle with walls and laws
and endless winding ways.

Lace up those gallant shoes and step into the street.
Lace up those impatient, leather-bound feet.
If you can see a road to any kind of liberty,

79

or hopeful peace that excludes defeat,
then run like lips that are too glad to say.
And do not concern yourself
with a road not taken –
your shoes have always known the way.

THE BIRTHDAY OF VENUS

We walked in the lee of limestone cliffs,
while the sea nudged lines of blackened weed
along an edge of churning foam –
shoving it out of itself – like an old stock of bitter words.
Chimes once spoken in the mumbling depths,
yet now, in the rapture of wind and wave – unheard.

There were rock pools too, where the stony feet of land
slung out of these ancient cliffs – etched anew –
milled by sea and weather – those unrelenting hands,
where the petrified edge of a waning flag
is chiselled back into diminishing shards.

We climbed the concrete steps then,
to get above the swilling tide –
up where the clifftop's sudden-edge,
is a blight of grass and imminent sky.
A last connection to the jealous sea,
torn to strings by its mithering heart –
then half-repaired by the rigorous gulls,
sewing its waves to this crack of land.

We saw a yacht out in the mist,
chopping slow in the sullen grey.
A vermillion sail – cut from a cloud of light –
that seemed a birthday card, or a beacon gift.
A devotion, to celebrate the birth of Venus
at this random persistence of map and chart.

And from those high cliffs, we sensed the sea
had summoned the tide of generous love –
and with the future spilt – or never meant to be,
it made her a present of all its shells.

I ASK, THEREFORE I AM

I am not a poet I am a human being
with a profound need to understand
where we are, where we are going –
and what the hell
we are supposed to be doing.

WE WILL ENDURE AS GHOSTS

The night is unravelled by wind,
with a full moon and a house full of sounds.
I am starting to think
we are still here.

LEAVE BURNING TORCHES TO SHOW YOU HAVE BEEN
Dedicated to the memory of Harper's Bookshop – circa 1970

1

We have sailed to the four corners of Earth
to find no other clue than puzzled people,
rowing back towards our silent face.
Sometimes with garlands and open hands,
other times without welcome, and frowned in menace.
Or wanting our mystery for their necessary gods.
Or wanting us gone; wanting us dead.
But we are all looking out for the same thing –
a covenant that none can readily define.
A pitch beyond the use of eager words –
discovery, adventure, travel... the sublime.

We sail on, side by side – outward and home,
reaching back with only suspicion to report.
A latent bargain no keen endeavour will recognise
now old-fashioned ears have long-since lapsed –
gone behind the exclusivity of dextrous lips –
a once-removed vocabulary of abandoned thought.

We explorers are cemented by a restless search –
looking for the same existential, yet invisible thing.

We call it experience or knowledge or power,
and use it as a sign, or a reference to draw on.

We attempt to trap this new burden of history
in the pages of books that trail their knowledge.
These are left open at our various stations
for passing eyes to penetrate and unhook –
to pick apart the threads of free and willing words
and make a language to sew into the cloth of maps.
We do this for the memory of ungoverned words,
whose legend of truth can only be heard
in the careful passing of a guided breath.

As in school, where we latched our critical words
under the lid of our secret space.
These juvenile ways were never abandoned –
the chewing gum and the carved initials,
or our unique experiments with sleeping bats.
These folded resistance into their shrouding wings –
an obdurate skin that is veined for energy –
making living lightbulbs for the science of darkness –
lamps for seeing unseeable things.

Humans are the archetypal thinking thing –

resting our pens on the fantasy of thought,
as though our ideas might become those of cherished scribes,
who turn ordinary words to art.

It is an untouchable thing,
and we are a colossus in a scribing world of ink.
Connected by chaos and the song of ourselves,
where thinking flows like an inspired nib –
an infectious prayer – or a random scribble.
Something not quite right and not quite here,
yet nonetheless, we are made aware
of this sentient pen –
sometimes gripped by the hands of spirits.
They spark in the darkness –
offering various permeations of care.
It resembles automatic writing –
flowing its aftermath into something good.

2

There is a similar marker for death now too.
Something witnessed in a casual mirror,
or revealed in a shop window as we steer by.
It is the wrapped bat of our guarded soul,
hanging under the lid of our hungry cave.

Here, in the land of our own graffiti,
we are in a contemporary place, as good as any,
but under scrutiny, and will not last.

Our lives will be recorded in the rays of the Sun,
and in the layers of the time-strung universe, yes,
        but hold on...
and stand your burning torches there.
Just in case our lives mark time as slipping frames –
        and see, my friend –
your marked location is already spent –
wasted on the overdrawn places of the past.
It slips behind your future name, and your last.

Whether in hope or despair,

shout to each other with a curved hand.

Like sailors out on passing ships –

"Who are we now and where?"

3

I will button my coat and explore my town.
The thirty-nine will bus me there – arriving full sail
into the crowded headlands of street facades –
the shops, the alleyways, the novel rewards.

And the haunted cobbles in All Saint's Square.

The bookshop is gone now, but who would care?
No one reads the obituary of knowledge,
killed by time and the death of words.
Knowledge has been replaced by the trivial union
of a consenting world in febrile disgrace.
The creeping factoids of popular culture,
that leggy octopus, wrapped around your phone.
And the near-death experience of social media.
A world you explored for half a day –
becoming at once, famous and unknown.

I will remember the bookshop and its glorious pages,
turning treadmill waves – reading through the ages.
And its windows, blowing in a gown of scrawl –
the rent sails of its noble struggle.
No doubt there is a new kind of virulent wind,
that blows against the breath of one and all.

Yes, the bookshop is gone now and who would care?
But just to confirm such gifts are precious,
I will light my torch and leave it there.

F. Scott Fitzgerald The Last Tycoon

F. Scott Fitzgerald The Great Gatsby

Nausea

Simone de Beauvoir

odern Short

Sartre Iris Murdoch

John Macquarrie/Existentialism

JOHN KEATS

Baudelaire Selected Poems

Laurens van der Post The Lost World of the Kalahari

Saul Bellow Mr Sammler's Planet

Albert Einstein RELATIVITY

the age of reason Jean-Paul Sartre

MARCUS AURELIUS MEDITATIONS

PLATO TIMAEUS AND CRITIAS

PART THREE

OBSTACLES

THE GHOST

My house is like a ship.
It creaks as I walk in its bowl of wood –
especially at night,
in the sea-quiet atmospheres
that fold thick and deep;
that haunt the air of plastered walls –
these sheer cliffs, painted white.

The journeys I make
are simple, yet profound.

One voyage takes me to a lower floor
to find a ship I hear-tell has run aground.
Its captain replaced by blesséd bone –
a shipwrecked sailor, swimming home.

And behind the noise
of all this wood and wave and stone...

I am a splash,
that otherwise makes no sound...

the last, lingering thought
of a persistence, unbound.

LOST IN THE NIGHT SHIFT
All looking for a way out of this sleeping-bag of nails

The derelict world at midnight, chimes full twelve.
She is the duchess of frightened men –
passing secrets in the black folds of voluminous hours;
widening the split veneer of our cultural guilt –
a righteous Earth, tending the shame of charity.

We accept that we are born again – but born still to die,
and without the casting-off of life's malingering betrayals.
I see a serious planet going crazy with its entrails –
all scissored short by the restrictions of duty
and the social betrayal of entrepreneurial thought.

It becomes a blessing now to ignore our fate,
and live beyond the scars of our countless wastelands.
The places where we robbed the depths of toil and sanity,
replacing deeps and narrows with abandoned sleep.

It is all marked on the hours of our watchman's brazier,
with the rumours of sex wrapped in unanswered seed.
But we were chasing nothing but unspecified desire,
and good-humoured are we, who watch the fire –
guarding time until the day-shift comes, clothed in dark.

A BIRD'S REACH

To be a bird is to feel the air, as fish feel the sea.
To be immersed in its fabric depths,
gliding beneath the blanket folds of an ocean sky.
Clouds roll as sea tides there, and hang like foam.

To be a bird is to look down on humankind.
To see us staring upward from our captive thoughts –
a jealousy pinned by a desire to fly...
or with some other ancestral quirk –
a hooked beak; an odd eye; a crested knot of hair –
a whistled tune, exempt from misery,
or from the need to even care.

Only a bird can see our longing to swim –
or to climb into the reaches of that nearest tree –
and on, into endless air.

HUMANS WITHOUT YOUR BLESSING

"What may not be expected in a country of eternal light?"
– Mary Shelley – Frankenstein.

"For every action, there is an equal and opposite reaction."
– Isaac Newton's third law.

What are they doing in secret laboratories –
hidden, unmapped and ungoverned?
Those suspicious mounds of bland earthworks,
blurred behind wind and planted trees.
Do you trust their concrete? You would be a fool.
They are replacing you with egg-mayonnaise –
stuffing it into the arms and legs of plastic bodies,
making compliant, pseudo-humans
who enjoy shopping even more than you – cyber beings,
who eat nothing that would cost the earth.
They chew on the short grass of a whittled economy –
living off the charitable shifts of zeroed work.
They service the playgrounds of the ungiving rich,
without complaint or tired eyes.
These utility beings, created in your image –
that of workers, consumers and random spillage,
are totally compliant and have no sense of injustice –
even when given plastic-bag-bodies
and the innards of a snail.

Before the legislation of replacement was passed
they tried to convert you into controllable beings.
But the complex details of your random thoughts
and your intangible longing for wish-filled days,
proved too elaborate for the sterile vacuum
of their one-track, silicone heart...

(its unsettling lack of diverse ways)

The experimental wires and endless extensions,
were unrooted cuttings that never seemed to take.
Your blood was too real for their synthetic tubes,
and no algorithms could deter the vision of roving eyes.
Nor the slight-of-hand of adaptable brains –
so randomly developed, through trial and error.

Now they have glass phials of coded genetics,
displaying a hierarchy of desirable skills.
They are mixing cowards for a brave new world –
creatures that might also resent their creators –
with their human silt and their tampering hands?

Perhaps not now, in this poor light of scientific glory,
but in the full and timely glare of shifting sands.

MY SECRET GARDEN

I have a secret garden which is locked.
It grows in the dark – forced like rhubarb.
It wreathes the house in swathes of ivy,
rooting into old books and the staircase steps.
It forms a green bannister to the upper floors,
where the Lord sits, dictating monstrous hours;
posting soft psalms into enduring ears;
latching the windows with creeping words.

His words are 'caustic' now
and that word frequently appears.
When I read them, they sting –
something trilling and sharp,
like soap in the eye.

The ivy trails on, through unmarked decades,
brown and dead in forgotten places –
the dry places that return to soil,
burying their labours in a code of rust.
It blooms in pockets of broken light,
or in the moisture of tears and uneasy toil.
It hangs on window frames, like Victorian lace,
trapping dust from the clouded night.

It binds everything with its creeping shade,
growing heavy in a snake-like twist.
It is a keeper of secrets – a silent momentum
that nothing has the polish to resist.

This whole house is a weave of roots.
They tunnel as veins to keep me alive.
Breathing independently of my own, ancient form,
which is ghost-like now and has lost its keys.

IN THE BACK OF MY CLOCK

i
I am awash with human noise at noon.
It runs down the windows like coloured rain,
and life haunts me as good as any ghost –
shrill and incomprehensible – incomplete.
A headless spectre – dark on Fridays.
Still frightening though – it has potential for fear,
as it burns in a breath of unsound air.

In need of security I hide in my clock,
becoming its natural, telling face.
Complete with Roman numerals
and a monocled expression –
taking the place of a lens, or an eye.
I pretend that time does not see me here,
inside its newly possessed hour –
here at the end of the beginning of time,
cloaked in clock-talk and quite at home.
I shiver though, throughout the day,
in the cold burden of this energy of dark.

ii
I think the world outside sounds apocalyptic,
with its death and real fire – its confusion and talk.

Yet I know, in their various schemes of oblivion,
these cackling humans merely dance their squawk.

Return them, O Lord, to their simple sanctuary –
a similar abode to my room in this clock.

iii
It was not always so for this reclusive mage;
with youth came the excesses of unqualified reach.
I danced with the confidence of Fred Astaire,
on my ebullient way into the wrath of the city.
I was flexible and thin – almost desirable –
and given the touch of a lightweight deity.
I walked my way in on a generous air –
skimming ideas like modern stones.
I shared the coloured ways of a rainbow bridge –
struck by Odin, in a northern grey.
And I have stolen these days from my own glad eyes,
and I have pressed them, like flowers
between the chimes of a clock.

When I was young, there was magic here too;
it rested, cradled in the buildings and the trees.

It haunted the air as a pale, white web
that kept us guessing – kept us busy –
sometimes it brought us to our knees.
It inspired us to attempt outrageous things –
and there was a sweetness there, I cannot describe,
as we moved from place to place – we charted beings;
feeling actually popular and almost required.
And I saw it there, this thin, white web –
it passed the windows on a teasing wind.
It blew across the carpark and shaped our cars;
it adorned the drunk of late-night bars.
It was more than a technicality – it was the spark.
It was a universal thread that knitted all life,
emerging from the opaque tar of a stranded ark.

iv
Talk and freedom were inseparable then –
unlike the threatening grunt we have today –
not the distressed ear, enfolded in cliché.
It was a realised language – discovered alone,
not just some processed talk – coded in a meme –
or a bandwagon offered in the liability of your phone.
It was a beautiful thing – an abandoned silence –
a dismantling of manufactured slang.

And now our lips are worded towards demise –
we must slide out of the lizard, to that better skin.

v

I acquired many books that lined my walls –
an insolation from the illegible world.
And well before the character inside this clock,
I built a tunnel of books and crept into that.
Crept into the narrowest, unprinted spine,
standing as tall and lean as I could –
stretching out thin and holding my breath.
I was paper then, but gnarled as wood.

I became a difficult book, none would read,
to avoid becoming a title of hope, or love,
or a national treasure – issued from above –
or a people's favourite, written in bed.
I was a zeitgeist pretending to catch on –
gratefully missed by the idealistically dead.

I avoided titles that hid in charity,
and are lost in the pretence of a cotton soul –
people always love the schadenfreude
and cannot resist a begging bowl.

I stuck to titles that contained fear and loathing,
though my favourite charade was poetry, of course.

vi
I was happy in this, my undiscovered world –
it was the only world I could bear to know.
Though in envy, I knew of other worlds,
and longed to visit their tempting pages –
those virgin plains – those great fields of snow.
I invited their souls to share my clock,
but they read from abandoned articles
I had long overthrown –
saying they were passages from my own lost books,
but I never wrote a book in my ancient life.
Nor a sentence, or a poem, or a note –
I never wrote a single letter,
or mumbled a clue in an optimistic quote.
And with this blind defiance, I showed them out.

It was fun, until it curved my brain
and dimmed my light.
Yet I suppose, it proved I could be usefully frivolous
in the interests of delight.

vii

Soon, I read out loud to the icy world,
and surprisingly they listened to my voice of snow.
They awakened from a sleep of frozen nations
to become 'one ear' for my private sound.
And although the chapters are all about me,
and there is little time left for anything else –
I can sense death breathing on my transparent face
and lighting a lamp in a distant world.

viii

There was a darkness in that hole – that cage of pauses,
where I decided to accept nothing
of the preceding ages.
Not even death – from which I had now risen,
as if a Lazarus, from a forgiving womb.

ix

So do not search for me with your torches and bibles –
I am solid stone now – made of mountains and rubble.
Nor with your thin pamphlets of holy redemption;
I have found better on my own ancient shelves.
I will only accept a journey to Bedlam
if it bears the disclaimer of: 'and part way back.'

But you can still read out words such as 'live or die',
and see how I feel about that...
yes, we can see how I feel about that.

X

At night, the mouth of the cave welcomes strangers
and is as bright as any soul you will find on Earth.
The mouth of the cave shines as a moon,
enhanced by an occasional, roving moth.
They dance against a background of ominous trees,
becoming sticks of light in these transactions of dark;
they are the animated fingers of my ceaseless clock,
and all the cogs behind us that prove our work.
They also mark the tradition of simple brotherhood,
and my heart is damp with everyman's blood –
It is as foul as congested midnight air,
passed one to the other with life's trailing kiss.

Who would be saved then – in that mutual terror?
In that act of relieving some disaster of breath?
It is life passed on in buckets to the unborn –
to the Holy Grail of the living fire.

xi

Inside my clock, I have manufactured stability,
yet it suits itself in times of need.
So I will tick here, until life's tsunami,
hits my darkening cave with a fall of breath,
returning this stolen province to the sea.

xii

Twelve o'clock, Twelve o'clock...

My clock has chimed for thee,
as it chimed for me.
I was blind at ten to two, deaf at five past three.
Lost behind the doors of a clockwork Noah's ark,
where we duplicate tomorrow,
with the winding of a key.

HUMAN GREED

Humans, in their need to survive –
always halfway to the stars
and feeling every minute alive,
will not survive their greed.

MY WILL

If I do not make it past this year,
then make this year a full stop
and move on.

THE BIG CLOCK

Meet me beneath the big clock.
The digital monstrosity you bought for our bedroom.
Big enough for the hordes of passengers and travellers
who tramp through our station of unscheduled dreams.
They are equally blind in the folds of solace –
either in our dark, curtained room
or the blur of their presence.

Let the giant clock be their arbiter of turmoil.

The four inch numbers construct their code
from a skeleton grid of arcane sticks –
like runes, or ancient cartouche bricks.
They glow in the night for passing ships
and illuminate our attempted equilibrium.

Numbers have a wonderful way with discipline;
they energise my mind as I try to sleep.
They keep me restless and awake,
taunting the hours with their accurate ridicule –
counting the rhythm of my unborn sheep.

They keep me engaged with a lucid obedience
to their rigid accuracy of abolished seconds.

And they never stray from their guardian grid –
turning up, as expected, like Immanuel Kant –
obsessively punctual to the point of snobbery.

We always seem short of time now –
with those big numbers chalking the days.
We know how long it takes to make the bed
or invent our necessary delays.
Or how many kisses have passed away
since we last boarded our Freudian train.

This clock has given us a new platform
from which to depart towards life's final edge –
everything current and sufficiently said –
the purity of rhythm and the music of numbers.

So meet me at midnight, beneath the big clock.
I will wear a carnation and one black sock,
so you can still recognise my stubborn impurities.

UNDISCOVERED POET

An undiscovered poet is a closed book –
an agony of heart that never opened out its truth,
and with all its pages glued shut.

I HAVE KNOWN STATIONS

I have known stations and their quiet benches,
expectant latitudes measuring the distance of trains.
I have known the derailment of emotion and thought
and the smoke, wrapped into my selfish cloud –
with its mumbling crowd of active ghosts.
And I have heard the silence in my waiting heart.

Among the ribbon-rails of dividing junctions
I have sunk into that substantial force –
bending the fabric of expired journeys
into the wrought-iron swirls of flowing miles.
I feel drawn into the dark of its infinity –
succumbed to its dangerous and alluring charm.
No sense of escape without unaffordable mercy,
but I feel freer in this moment than I have felt before.
The world cannot expect more from surviving souls.
We have done our worth and boarded our trains.
We have walked away from our theatre of light,
with no need of a script or stage door.

There will be time enough to struggle out
of these giddy bones –
to make-sail towards a port of reincarnated life.
But there is no discovery in this particular minute,

'I Have Known Stations': continues...

and no need for rumours or inherited strife.
I am not Columbus, and these are shallow voyages,
where I might happily run aground.
Or come abrupt, against a buffer-stop of experience –
a determinative siding in which to park my voyage.

Here in the pale and perfect dust of light –
I refuse to invest in empirical tricks,
just to own another mile of perfect mistakes.
Or to climb to the top of all I have known –
to stand at the highest and most desolate alone –
and then to fall into the calm suds of another birth
and the closed eyes of comfortable sleep.

I will push, once more, through the tunnel of my being,
urging my blood to form that ramrod of power.
Packing fuel into the next big bang –
that tiny star of everything.
It fires blood into future lives – beyond the scenes
of awkward and uncomfortable scripts.
Scenes that are shaped so badly they snap,
yet defy all logic and make positive sense.
They will be gathered into the welcome of experience.

I will meet old girlfriends in the street
and find my ancient energy rising in their smile –
flying as a raven through a path of light –
a remembrance of those rich and turbulent days,
when we fused our perfection in a grateful dance.

I will take these moments inside my heart.
I will carry them in my luggage, carefully packed.
I will not consign them to the dust of the past
with labels or diaries or missing parts.
And I will not look back –
for I have not yet finished with any part of my life.

My network of rails is the work of my bones,

they reach back in time, with their contorted efforts,

to grab the last desire of an unturned stone.

There are unmeasurable aeons in universal thought,
and if I snatch at them all it will break the code.
So I have learned how to rest – to wait it out.
I know how to reach that patient state,
in the unbearable eternity
between unknown stations.

THE AWKWARD DAYS OF MISADVENTURE

 I had a cold day – out of touch –
and people getting in the way.
Or was that me – out of sync and well astray?
The wounded me, abroad in a world
that sometimes does not seem to see.
But why, if they see themselves do they not see me?

While in the street, I think myself a ghost –
timing is so important and so cruel.
I end up displaced or derailed
or just feeling like a fool –
a sudden limp, where I had no limp –
unable to disengage from the dizzying flow
of head-on strangers, passing by –
is this the same for many...

       or just I?

There are demons in the world, for sure –
and they endure in the currents
of these, our flowing streets.
And in the ebbing tide of our subtle failings.

THE SILENT STROKE

I heard it first, that silent stroke of midnight.
I heard it before the machine,
with its ruthless measuring of my brain –
slicing the image, frame by frame.

So I am here, with the sword of Damocles
resting on my patient skull,
and part way in.

THE IMPOSSIBLE FOSSIL

1
We found it in the dried-up bones of an old river bed –
a ribbed channel from ancient times; a patience
that had turned its head to the languor of antiquity,
piling treasures to be marooned and smothered
in the eventual folds of its silt and mud.
Then the shallows of indifference advanced
and lay down the layers of years, like cake.
It went unsliced or misunderstood,
until the ancients carved a temple there,
smeared with the disparity of high civilisation
and ritual blood.

An aeon had buried our relic's head –
a great stone skull of replaced bone.
It was lost in the bigger brain of inexhaustible time,
beneath the bedevilled imaginings of frightened men.
We cannot see beyond the smallest years
and all else is a rubber band –
it stretches backward out of hand,
twisting taut its infinite beginnings.

Our own age sits on that same, vile step –
the monstrous fossil of our own doing.

We compress light beneath an insidious throne –

    built on ruin.

We are a bird of prey, reduced to prayer –
the king condor of polluted air;
a skunk in a bin that will not scare,
smearing the cream of fanning lies.
We buried our love with the spade of mayhem
and ignored the prophecy of darkening skies.

We dug deep to undermine ourselves.
We dug to find and to define ourselves –
to carry a soiled Earth upon our backs
and bear that disturbance as our home.
We did not come too late – we 'became' –
and each of us arrived alone –
our souls drying into threadbare rags,
and that was the shame.

There was a reverence of yearning
in those willing, human eyes –
a definite affection for this magical,
yet ultimately cruel surprise.

'The Impossible Fossil': continues...

So now we look back to other ages,
unreasonably chafed by blame and guilt.
And always searching for the victim, or the crime
or the heralded catastrophe,
upon whose early hours of false instruction
our broken road was so lately built.

2
The discovery of the giant skull
came at a pause in our expedition.
We had fed like wire into the jungle's heart,
with its teaming gifts that no one wants
and the dangers that drip from sulking trees.
We found the temple beneath a neglected seat,
as we rested our ruins on an old, vacant throne.
Its measure had suddenly removed a shroud
from the weary eyes of our trodden ways –
and via the miraculous expedient, of god-forged rays.

Light poured down like streams of sand,
through the canopy's clock of leafy cloud.

We listened to the garbled voices of ancient gods,
assertively cut into these telling blocks of stone.

Their robust presence in that precise air
filled us with neither benefit, nor distain.
Students and professors began to speak them aloud,
while we could not understand a word they said.
It was as if our scholars had become fervently zealous,
or by some lost inheritance, had fallen willingly insane –
their lungs enraged with the long breath of testament,
in the sudden audience of awakened deities.

It was a risk to peer beyond our limited interpretations;
to scrape off the moss and speak them aloud.
It is like listening to English without its noble key –
there are just too many overlapping sounds;
too many old struggles in that age-blurred stone;
too many concerns that mean opposing things.

3
At the heart of our discovery came the triumph:
the temple was built on a splinter of rock –
a foundation stone – a guiding foot – or so we thought.
It held a code only the crudest men could crack –
those never trusted with care – who never look back;
not predisposed to the joy of knowledge;
not in tune with the joy of anything.

These men were thieves and rapists of a new Babylon
and had hardly drunk their tea
before their hammers were unleashed.
They spit shards of rock at their own identity,
and were fully in contempt of their splitting blades.
It was as though the sharp side of their own tools
had rebelled against their pillaging hearts.
In truth, their only lament was in thoughts of home,
as they beat their frustrations out of their work.

These war chisels knew nothing of the past
and were half unconscious by midday.
By then, in reward for the sacrifice of time
much progress had been made.
The ground was swept into dry piles of silt.
The rock then lay defined as a hollow vault –
an empty drawer, stained with shadows;
sealed by hands loyal to the earliest of gods,
or by an endorsing priest with a sainted presence?
It was the brain cavity of a giant skull – a hollow bell –
a clapped-out note of appalling quiet,
that had rung out its years in terrible silence.
A temple-sized cabinet of perished prayers?

We could not tell...

Those who might have sown a clue inside their being
had sealed their mouths and eyes with dust.
They were set asleep on a course for quiet
and well within the tolerance of oblivion.

4
The megalithic bone is a trophy of imbalance;
an incomplete source of new perusal.
It is destined for the hungered eyes of palaeontologists,
set to stew in the flesh of unfathomable instances.
It is a ponderance for the dry meat of archaeology –
that gaping puzzle of wonder and impotence –
a confounding spark of long lost energies,
too eagerly charged in the pulse of museums.
It is a library from the past, with so few words
it can no longer provide its own meaning –
this relic, now annotated as: 'the work of ghosts' –
and 'extinct minds from a foreign caste'.

With our current words we cannot know
what thoughts they shared – those people there.
Or what creations were purely pleasure,

in their unique exploration of timely air.

These moments are now set back and trodden in –
or sometimes stubbed out by technical error.
Yet well beyond the selfish measure
of our doubtful human triumph.

We are well forward of the fevered labour
of their chiselled words and what they represent.
For who knows what they thought or cared,
or might have individually meant...

when they were living women
and living men?

PART FOUR

ENCRYPTIONS

A FUSION

Finally, after all our years had washed ashore,
we merged as long shadows on the windy promenade.
Two fish, swimming home from the harbour wall,
with a catch of humans, twisted in our net.
All the people we could not let go –
if not quite ever, then not just yet.
We had worked them into the beauty
of our bipartisan disguise.
They blended well in most weathers –
with our ordinary words and our mutual sighs.
Particularly with the sun behind our thoughts
and a daylight moon behind our eyes,
as we pushed north, arm in arm,
to catch our breath as living shadows.

BEYOND THE DOOR

It is not easy to look like hazardous waste,
you have to give up everything you know,
including your family – although by now,
they would not weep to see you go.

You grow your hair a little stranger,
with no bearing on aesthetics or style.
You shuffle between doorways,
gates and houses – and sleep in soil.

You are a vagrant to the polite –
and trash to the insecure.
You have rights they cannot bear,
and they cannot bear the poor.
Yet you do not wear anything
that you did not own before –
not a hat, not a coat, not a glove,
nor a horn, or a claw –
the only thing missing is a door.

Romantically, you have the stars –
in death, you have the breath of cars.
They burn your steps on trails of fire,
heating the verge in the turmoil of spring.

Bleeding heat into unweeded grass
and into the edge of everything.

You will never starve or feel the cold –
your mind has adjusted to reject all pain –
you have trained your young self to be old
by reaching too far into the insane.

There are few questions to ask anymore,
and the road is already too far to inquire.
But where does the next hour come from –
and how will it travel –
without purpose or desire?

A FATAL SIGH

Death chases me around the house.
I go from room to room to shake it off.
I try to occupy my bag of gloom
with minor thoughts – with indifferent things.
This becomes that, as the light rolls through,
cutting an arc made of glass and shadows –
the long fingers of scribing time.

Outside, in autumn light, I hear a voice or two;
rambling lips, warbling out some common news –
dead gossip that does not need care –
a reassuring preamble of ubiquitous despair –
the collective covenant of human amplitude.
Gossip passes the time though, and lifts the air,
like hammering hot rivets into a cold ship.

Inside the house despair is different;
despair is humble, and resembles coal.
It has become the subject of my pseudoscience
that even the deepest physics cannot explain –
questioning its dark energy and mistrust of time.

       Then the clocks all stopped at once,
       while my hands moved on

with subservient feet and a mindful eye –
trying not to collide with my wavering fate,
yet then, being off-guard, I hesitate –
        I disengage; I sigh.

And that is when suicide's quotation marks appear,
fixated on where I am and why.
They say my name between wolves' ears –
or words forged in iron, behind a setting sun.
Those suddenly shallow, insipid seconds
that would have ticked mercifully on –
they stick now, like all the stopped processions –
        here... and nigh.
And there is a knock on every door –
on every whispering floor. In every space or staircase,
from the clouded attic to the dead cellar step –
where light bends back
into the Victorian black it was before.

Death is my mother now,
and I, in my dark doubt, am revealed.
Suicide's hand has called me down
to brush my hair; to set me free –
a boy again – heading off to school.

FOR ROBERT LOWELL: CLASS 222

If anyone comes late to my class
or if anyone comes at all,
tell them I will be in room 222.
Class begins in 1958,
in the Fall.

FLESHING OUT A POEM

Poetry is the most beguiling art –
its luring question is when to begin.
A decision prompted by sirens and angels
or a torturous prodding until you give in.
A message from God to the almost insane?
A crowd of clerks sifting files in your brain?
An intrigue; a deluge; a rose; a pain –
you can let them go, or get a pen,
but if you get a pen…

everything you were doing
will uncouple its train.

Once begun, the bones of a poem
will strive to become your improbable twin.
Demanding to be sewn into the thread of your veins
and the cloth of your skin.

LEAKED WORDS

I tried to listen, but sensed your words were fake,
so I heard only sounds that had no true meaning.
Since then, I have tried to memorise this poem;
to make a record of my attempts to listen –
and also as evidence of our various conversations.
I thought it might prove useful in a world of lies
and I now know these words off by heart –
these words that have no true meaning,
even as I speak them out.
They do not even sound like words anymore –
they sound slippery and guarded – more like eels –
more like doubt.

Speaking your congealed words, I sound deceitful,
just as you did before you died.
I picture myself with the same, green head,
with its hair of snakes writhing on the ground –
each snake a word and each word a sound
and each letter spoken with a forked tongue.

Rest easy in your mammoth death,
your deceptive words are safe with me –
they still mean nothing that holds a truth,
so do not fear a finding out.

I have decided not to write them down
because I cannot write with a forked tongue...
and I would never betray your liar's heart,
nor stain your ruthless words with ink...
      but my publisher might –
he has a certain kind of impish wink
and never listens to a word I say.

PLASTIC HEN

I saw a plastic hen.
I cannot remember where or when.
It is a vision that will not come to mind
and alleviate the fear of having lied –
lied to myself with my own eyes.

There is a nagging uncertainty now –
it coils around me like a snake,
trying to crush the truth out of a possible mistake –
that the hen I saw was real – and not a fake –
complete with feathers and a nostrilled beak.
Did I see a breeze blow through its wing?
Did I see it peck at just about anything?
Did I hear it speak?

Did I really see a plastic hen or was it just a plastic pen?
I could tap at a page then, or write like a beak –
peck at words that make no sense –
become a plastic-feathered freak –
add writing to my plastic plate with poison ink?
I could drink new words and spit out a page.
I could write a critique in a pecking rage.
I could join the hen-house of the local paper,
where peacocks scratch the dirt all day,

scooping the stony lies of egged-on news –
headlines hatched from febrile gossip.

I would become part of the 'Daily Hen',
and be aloof inside their plastic bubble
that shits out print at half-past ten.
I could do the night-shift without any stars.

But what does the plastic editor say?
Does he tell me what to think and do?
Does he tell me what I saw in a street near Waterloo,
while I was chasing down a slowly cooling scoop?
Does the editor re-speak my words
to say I'm wrong?

I have become a plastic hen now.
I have become a plastic pen now...

and I am riding home on the midnight-bus
through a blizzard of sudden snow.
I tap at the window or at a can of Coke.
I tap with my impatient plastic beak
that bounces off my iPhone like a cruel joke.
It becomes a window I cannot quite open;

'Plastic Hen': continues...

mirroring a chicken I cannot place.

I tap on my door with my beak of lost keys
and I am instantly turned away –
my long-term partner has revealed she is gay...

I kneel before her – stretched like cling-film
over a nervous parcel of doubt –
as a writer, I am a man of plastic letters –
and to her: "a fucking bastard plastic lout".
I have no control over my own news now,
I am just trying to avoid being edited out.

I am a plastic bag with nothing in it –
a plastic hen, or at best, something small and feathered,
and pitifully dead – a frozen Linnet?
Something that might dry in the spring and blow away.

To her, I am only frozen sperm –
no longer part of sexual desire
but maybe useful in the long term.

She turns to the dog and says:
"I can't believe what I just saw.

There was a plastic hen knocking on our door –
an empty hen, with no use or substance –
transparent and hollow: like sunglasses, only darker.
I am not even sure it was a hen,
or a crow, or just a claw...
but I probably know what I saw...
Yes, I know what I saw."

The dog is no help and is cowering now –
as I cower too on our frozen steps.
A headless chicken in a partnership of the blind,
where we can only see our broken eggs.
She knows there is someone there though
and whispers aside,
stepping back through the open door, saying:
"I thought I saw a plastic hen,
I just cannot remember where, or who, or when."

TRAVELLING LIGHT

I passed in a car, with the rain hissing at its blur –
someone else driving,
which is always the lesser way for me.
I like to drive, I like to see... but not too much.
I see the concentrated look ahead and little more.
I let the rest swipe past my mind,
reflected in the science of a polished door.

As a passenger I see too much –
like rolling an eyeball down the street –
a viscous world sticking to its searching feet.
But not today – today I saw some good:
two ladies stood on a pavement edge,
their umbrellas curving a roof-space from the storm.
Each identity locked into this mutual hood.
They whispered some new gossip
that washed with the world into a gulping pool.

Perhaps they spoke of absurd husbands,
or some new telling of an old pain?
Or the whispered condemnation
of a threatening neighbour – suddenly insane?

But it was not for me to trouble these thoughts.

I was merely placed to continue by,
in all this uncertain certainty –
where one anonymous, whispered word
could cause an elemental sigh.
For we were all a concoction of light and atoms,
randomly drawn, in that moment of a day,
where the ladies' pink faces shone as blossom,
in a vast field of teeming grey. And I?
I was travelling towards the rumour of God –
being delivered, in a way.

THE PAST IS SO SAD

The past is so sad, yet unappreciated in its time.
It leaves us stranded in a soured future,
looking back at what we had;
looking back through closed windows
we will never now get to open –
pitilessly locked in an obstinate lifeline,
and the continuing error
of a path, unbroken.

CO-REDEMPTRIX
The Difficult Contradictions of Love

If a woman loved, worships Jesus Christ,
and is worshipped herself, in a sincere way,
is it ever possible to be in the sight of your saviour,
without complete deference and eternal faith?
I offer this thought as a plausible argument
for my inexplicable display of inadequate loyalty,
and the undeniably cordial outcome
of an inconclusive divorce.

TURNING THE YEARBOOK
Winifred's Garden towards Autumn

There are long shadows across the lawn
at only 4.00pm.
And even with this evidence
of a continuing summer sun
there is a coolness about the air –
autumn seems begun.

The trees are nudged-up and proud,
but there is a sepia stain
in their rippling shroud.
And eyelid flowers droop and fall,
becoming rare.

There is a stilted limp in a butterfly's flight,
that oscillates like a failing machine.
But even with winter hiding
less carefully in the ground,
everything is right.

SUMMER WITH THE GODS
Passing Like Paint Through Creative Rooms

I tried to think of things I could do for you
but there was nothing, so I did nothing.
I pondered in a dangerous chair,
surrounded by traitor notes and winking scribes,
and the details of imagery – that fire of ideas –
theoretical solutions to real lives.
These were offered to the customers of our clients;
perceived as aspirations and expected joy.
People were bored with the old ways of thinking,
and sought new ways to think the same things.
Such was my precarious ledge of being,
amid the perfect imperfections of advertising.

Our life became enmeshed in this golden dawn
and leant into the anguish of unnecessary burden.
I was hooked out of my simple-self and enthroned:
an acting hierophant – a guru of the uncertain.
I was caught between distance and disconnection,
where the unimpeachable voice of a perfect love,
lay lost on the slopes of a shaded valley –
where I was plagued by the curse of the beggar-king;
my stone tower becoming the seal of sacrifice –
a ritual involving everything.

My secret potions – mysterious, even to me –
remained a strong, creative source –
yet seemed no more than identifiable flavours,
kept aloft in accessible jars.
I could take them down from a nearby shelf
and put them back again, like a bag of sweets.
I could drag them out with confident strokes
and blend a new era of beckoning change.
All beyond the background of our troubled hours,
and our slipping embrace.

There was no shelf of ideas for you and me.
Our advertisements lived in awkward surprise –
these formal proclamations that no one believed,
such as eulogies and epigrams – forgivable lies.
Our own folly crept out into the loudest letters –
a tragic, mumbling, menacing machine.
We could question our course of daily disturbance,
but never quite change our uncertain minds.
It was the truce of those ads that admit defeat,
but only with a warning and no call to action.
Their smokers knew their own truth anyway,
and could not care less about accepted warnings.
They wondered what took the authorities so long

to finally confess a mutual secret –
just as we knew, in the ache of our hearts,
no escape was necessary from our permanent bond.
Not without impossible abstentions from each other,
or the depth of our enduring loyalty of love.

There was no way we would stub each other out.

Through the next long years, when nothing happened,
except rolls of imagery for drooling eyes.
And the sea waiting it out, on its prowling tide.
And trees stepping forwards of their rooted place –
these monstrous weeds of suburbia and city,
that proved mercy could grow, or be allowed to happen,
in this complex sludge of roots and rain.

I became unstable then – in the glamorous sunshine –
and in the pain and miracles of searching turmoil.
As a fish grows bored in its mirrored bowl –
endlessly swimming without destination,
or the conviction to change the direction of the shoal.
I was looking inward to myself too long,
and life was becoming surprisingly dark.
The only escape seemed in the colour of autumn,

which advanced on the gossip of absconding leaves.
Then the rumours came – pointing a way out –
an inviting door from this game of rooms.
And as the Sun grew short of daily breath,
and with no external wind to ruffle my fears,

      I cast myself out...

I flew in the face of every god,
and with some... though very little doubt.
I walked away from a stage I had built,
and where I had finally chosen to forget my lines.

I was struggling with thoughts and blatant obsessions –
designs for which, there were no coloured pens.
I closed the layout-pad of this created life
and walked a different road instead.
It was a withdrawn path of deep contemplation,
but alas, no compass for travelling home.

Yet it proved a road of miracles and goodwill,
often guided by your loyal and impeccable grace.
There were many diversions along the way
and I seemed to drift through them – a popular ghost.

I was passing like paint through creative rooms,
where my clients invariably endorsed my work –
even with these self-inflicted, baggage-car-wounds
scarring an undeniably transparent host.

I came and went – a sailing ship,
on many seas and many tides.
Without chart or reason – and minus sails –
I was a ghost-ship – running on the fuel of fire –
a clipper, scorched by the burning cloth
of unredeemable love and unholy desire.

I have yet to arrive home after all these rooms;
with all their plaudits and their billowing sails.
And I am clutching the edge of a running tide –
still at the mercy of wind and wave.
Yet after all these years, I cannot accept
that our story is told behind a speeding stern,
so I have wandered back into the craft of letters,
that will visualise my dereliction,
in uncharted words.

SELF ELEGY

Only you know now,
because I am dead.
Only you know where we sat
and listened
and said.

PART FIVE
REPRISALS

DECLARATION OF WAR AND PEACE

I have an army who say they will follow me to hell.
I tell them every day that we are not marching to hell,
but they do not listen – they like to feel reckless –
a crumbling fortress – a torn carcass –
a rampart of smoking bricks with handprints of blood –
fingerprints discarded as rumours of death.

They want to die in a remembered valour;
illustrated in a book and toasted by historians.
Yet a tome of words, where not a page is pompous –
these men long to die with their boots unpolished –
awarded posthumous medals – flavoured with guns.

We must declare our enemies as they have declared us.
If only to appease our soldiers and their resting talons.
To keep them wretched and insanely focussed;
to allow them to dream of our impassioned intentions
and to ponder the considerations of uneasy glory.

All this is well enough, until we map the next battle –
the bloodier campaign, that will dwell on the past –
shuffling resentfully, towards a declaration of peace,
with its unavoidable reprisals for comrades lost.

A CROWN OF BONE

There will be another life for me –
this one is old and bitter.
A rusting throne of metal thorns
where I am seated and shut.
A king who stands for nothing –
unopposed – more likely forgotten.
About to abdicate
into the periphery of death.

Freedom was lost in the chains of its privacy.
Justice squandered on the price of pity.
I swept the fingers of pilfering politicians,
clouding their urge for glittering dust.
I sealed their oily mouths with suffocating sand.
I hung their mockery of common sense.
All there is to do now,
in the vile introspection of a sovereign state,
is wait... while pretending not to repeat myself
or hesitate... or hesitate...

My reign is over, is the simple truth;
a closed bandwagon on a rusted siding.
Sealed forever, I have been shunted to my fate.

My crown of bone has no translucent skin –
the peach-purity of its youthful soul.
It sits atop an anguished, pale and brooding thing,
fissured with the deep cracks of nagging years.

But there will be another life for me,
beyond the petty bounds of unconquered land or sea.
Everything soothes in the balm of time,
when refused the misery of brutal failure,
for the simple beauty of common decline.

IT IS COMING

It is coming – with the dark side of your holy book:
the civil war; the unrest; the apocalypse;
the fabled Armageddon.
The busy afternoon of bedlam –
that mad march through your town centre
while you are simply out shopping.
Thugs with bottles, smashing the pavements;
glass everywhere, except in your glasses –
trodden underfoot.

The monster is on your doorstep now,
as the casual slice of teatime approaches.
Leaning on your passage wall; swinging on your gate.
As threatening as a giant – as unsettling as an ant –
an assassin, lighting a cigarette –
to burn the last minute of your fate.

It is almost time to silence your clock,
for everyone's tick has a final tock.
It checks its watch to make doubly sure
that death's simple chime is neither fast, nor poor.
It will soon light the fuse on a cartoon bomb
and blow its own head into a black, sooted ball,
with the orbiting stars of kingdom come –

and yours too – and everyone.

We will all continue then, refreshed and unscathed;
skipping off into the next paradise.
This takes the form of a fresh, unclouded frame –
as predicted in the animated words
of your suspicious book.

BEHIND THE EYE

The eye looks inward,
asking questions never asked of the beyond –
that far infinity in front of our face;
a painted veil, wearing thin.

Behind the eye is more interesting;
more of a puzzle, and a harder world to fathom –
even harder to let yourself in.
You will not need a key, just a clumsy hairpin –
you can fiddle with that until a lock gives way;
until a gate swings open or a barricade falls,
or an open window reveals the weakness of walls.
Or you can lean on your doubt until it breaks –
crawl through the cat-flap of your naïve mistakes
into the basket-case that is the social life
of your kitchen.

Armageddon begins here –
amongst the mess of lepers and unclean dishes;
amongst the sliding panic of magnet-clad fridges
that grip the instructions of essential truth:
those random notes and bestowed best wishes.
Here, amongst the five loaves and a pair of fishes,
is the delinquent energy of rotten fruit –

unsliced, withered – a true crucible of universal fire
that you could not set your mouth to smother;
even with its ramble of extinguishing words –
it is a still life of knives – with spores and bacteria.

Now, in this valley of death, you grow doubtful too.
But never mind, set the kettle to pour another brew –
celebrate your own insanity coming to the boil.
This is always unsettling – even as an idea –
even as a recipe, left open for others;
a note of suicide; a poem for lovers;
an early photograph of your abandoned self.
Yes, we know you would rather be someone else,
but there is no backdoor behind the eye –
it is as far as you can go to escape your veneer.
And even then, you will meet some new dark thing,
solely purposed to unfold in your ear.

THE ENTROPY OF A LARGE HOUSE

The walls of my house are eaten by scrawl –
lines of spider-wire that are beginning to extrude;
etching figures of newly born sentience,
that explain time's skill at wrapping the aeons.

They assume the shapes of ancient drawings –
echoing the first poems of human existence;
painted as witness to the shapes of living;
daubed on this new cave of murderous history.

CLICK

Our time is a ratchet.
It ticks on, latching the seconds;
a tight grip of moments, cog to cog.

We cannot step back –
each moment tightens on the last...
until something breathes out
and there is a crack.

It is a mistake we cannot learn from –
cannot unmake – an injured moment
we cannot build again, or fake.

We realise then... we are trapped –

locked in a forward gear that aches and aches;
longing for the soul of safeties past
and their comfortable legions of folded days.

We are undone – un-cast –
with the stack of each relentless century
caught behind the last.

CRICKET

Out beneath the spread-rafters of another age,
the white-men linger across their pitch of tribes.
Bowling an avalanche they cannot catch –
well beyond the batsman's physical stare.
He churns the ball in a heated second
into the blue powder of a comfortable sky.
Then silence slides back to its heavenly order,
as these flanneled-men reshuffle discretion
into the fear of another flighted ball.

LADY PACROVEAN MEETS HER MATCH

Madam, I am tired of your lies.
They are woven in the tresses
of your creature hair.
You stink of other men
and put me down.

Those trees in your garden –
I will climb them in summer.
Hide in their leaves
and pretend to be no one.

I will ripen a smile amongst emerging fruit.
Let you discover me, naked –
yet tasting of bitter.

EYES THAT SEE AND KNOW

In the silence before we speak,
everything we are going to say is said.

Ears do not need to listen,
having stared at our thoughts with knowing eyes –
with the human handling of fabric and scenery,
all weighed with the precision of balanced scales.

And all with the borrowed assembly of skilful souls,
maintaining the cosmos
with unseen tools.

They usher in our unsaid words
through the gaping portal
of listening eyes.

THE MOON CONTROLS US

The Moon controls us – she controls the sea –
that well of ink that scribes the shore,
writing its tales of evolving genes.

Once they whispered in the curdled throws
of an unexpected chemical birth –
drawing up the genesis of you and me.

We were written into the world by water and by air,
and although we cannot see the sorceress Moon,
in this shrouded cloud of night's glare,
we know by the tides of our obeying blood –
she is there.

THE HOLLOW MOON

The Moon is industrial – a landscape of work.
She gathered up her dust in a fist of gravity,
slipping into quiet exhaustion
as the last shift fell on an easy breath.
This was the Moon's heroic era,
before she froze her cemented face
into a night-time sun of precious light.
Her stone machinery clicked silent then,
after many bombarding aeons of toil.
They had scribed out her patterns and her plans
into a baked prospect, more of dust than rock or soil.
A crater here; a dry sea there –
an unrelenting livery of grey.
An impeccably defined trust of light and shade,
cast by a glamorous sun and its paramour, night.

They say the Moon rang like a bell,
one haunted evening in nineteen-seventy –
as though the black stone of a reverberating thought
was dropped into a listening well.
But she was merely sending her workers home
at the end of the last, enormous shift –
these, her tired and invisible ghosts,
that the bouncing boots of astronauts had cut adrift.

The Moon is never redundant though,
she moves with the majesty of control and time –
musing oceans and our similar ways
with fluid commands, born in a science of chimes –
These dutiful ambitions are set fluid deep,
in the brooding tide of our liquid hearts.

AUTUMN HIGHLIGHTS

Your hair is like wood – neat, but cut with an axe;
bark scraped off the sides, with a chiselled look –
deftly applied by an up-swept blade.
You scent it with spray,
as if any respectable young tree would bend to care –
young trees swoon to the sway of a breeze,
or pour their face of leaves into an autumn wind.
They are not lured by tricks with hair.

Your hair is unmoved by unsociable wind –
as the trees are unmoved by your galant hair.
A new look for spring, designed in winter,
when your friends made a campfire
of your arrogant sweepings –
"Just to keep our hearts warm," they said,
while watching you work in the glow of memories,
and with a mild appreciation of your brute form.

And why not? You were bare-chested in firelight –
soothed, warm, and wielding an axe at your own head.
Such scenes are rare, even in the life of a troubadour.

Their minds cast back to when you were a sapling
with a talented body made of lyres –

a lithe stem that you were obliged to share,
strumming out your summer aspirations
on the staves of their branches.

Did they love your limbs – slender in the wind,
better than this rigid and distracting hair?
Have they noticed your autumn highlights creeping on,
like streetlights in the afternoon – one by one –
called to bear witness to deciduous wear and tear?

Have they noted that your skin is becoming bark?

When you are old and your hair grows white and thin,
peeling like the skin of a silver birch,
I will weave your name into the receding quiff,
and watch the fingers of advancing frost,
outline your stylish ideas of arboreal fashion
and its valiant attempts at seasonal romance.

ROOTED IN THE SAP OF BLOOD

There is a plot that weaves through autumn days,
informing blood with its whispered strands,
and daylight is shutting down its market stall –
wrapping its goods with careful hands –
sweeping night into piles of shadows.

The trees have felt a cooling air,
urging seasonal intent into extended fingers.
And on this paradigm of ancient perils,
have abandoned their leaves, and are growing south.
They rummage into the roots of their ordered keep,
and while cutting off the fraying end of a sliding summer,
they withdraw their canopy into a fall of sleep.

We humans withdraw from each other too,
when the sensibilities of pleasant smiles
seem untimely as forbidden love –
frowned upon by the sinking folds of cautious light
that weeps from all around – from the hallows of above.
It is a hardship that we lighten, as we may –
opening a book – pulling on a glove.

Actors need the absorbing light of spring and summer;
a full, unfolding scene behind our pitch and stall.

A whole theatre, wrapped into a peacock's tail –
with the slight of hand of a fanning shawl.
A momentary clock that ticks its second
restoring blood into a waking age –
a fusing of confidence and resistant joy –
the undeniable sense of a turning page.

Until then – and regardless
of who or what may attempt to sing,
we turn off our desires
and their beacon light,
till spring.

CROWS ON THE BEACH

Crows on the beach are different birds.
Even in sunlight their darkness never goes.
They are the black angels of an abandoned curse,
pecking at shells in a dark inquiry.

Sweeping in, with crossed shadows,
they drew a crucifix on this palm of sand.
Then a trance overcame my wavering soul
and I saw myself dead – crucified:

I was an offering to the pangs
of a kindred humanity –
harsh, yet without question,
I would abide.

I was still breathing on this slip of light,
with visible breath, as cold as snow.
And with no heat from the yearnings of a scribing sun
I asked the sky to let me go.
I prayed for tides to wash my being –
for clawing waves to rake my shadow.
And for this polarisation of light and shade
to merge into a single burning arrow.

Then all the religions of the world caught fire
and were extinguished as one, by a peaceful god.
And the universe collapsed into a crumbling pyre,
with its ancient sand and its aeons of flood.
And what remained was a luminous beach,
with a glowing horizon out in the reach.
There were no stars in this new order of light,
only mumbling particles from a difficult science –
a quantum physics of shimmering illusion,
tuned to pass our blueprints on.

The crows fell silent then
and seemed gone.

But they had hidden themselves
in adopted shells,
and felt at home.

THE OBELISK: 2021
I found an obelisk like the one in 2001: A Space Odyssey.

1

Braving the windswept beach and resembling Odysseus,
which was my natural look then – a noble stance,
I carried the visionary grace of a renowned hero,
yet some saw me as a vagrant with a glazed expression.
This is often unavoidable in the life of an adventurer
and quite beneath any thought of rebuttal.

It was then that my summer eyes saw the great marvel,
resting upright in a scree of pebbles.
An obelisk, much smaller than it appears on film –
and settled gratefully in the palm of my hand.
Never-the-less, I was deep in reverence,
it being a muse of universal mystery and power.

I invited scientists, scholars and holy men
to break with tradition and visit my house.
An attempt to communicate with its black infinity,
where all faiths and disciplines were welcome, of course.
And in the troubled beauty of a self-complicating world,
almost every denomination agreed to attend.
They were mostly concerned that the magic of heresy,
both scientific and religious, was about to be cast –

a crime requiring their intrinsic condemnation
and their expertise on the statutes of civil control.

The scientists were soon at odds with each other,
glowing with greed, as much as discovery.
The holy men prayed beneath agile breath,
that 'blasphemy' would serve to strengthen their calling.
And surely their god was great enough with words
to contradict any enlightenment offered in stone?

They gathered around the anomaly to observe,
yet it did not flinch from its wondrous form.
It stood six centimetres tall, and perfectly lit –
having gained two spotlights and a key light for drama.
All these scouring eyes, raking for trouble,
in a combination of doubt and light,
gave the obelisk an aura of incomparable majesty
that commanded the attention of the unsettled room.
It was like watching Marlene Dietrich, singing in a bar –
the same edgy atmosphere of worship and doom.

It was a black beast of unknown power –
an untapped potential of benefit or death?
And all had a clear view of its dark workings,

Witnessed by these critics as a blank stare.

There was a silence then –
the very moving silence of baffled men.
And at least three of us began to weep –
this being an undeniable fusing of unity and hearts –
It was science and gospel, pretending to be humble,
behind a preference for fame and wealth.

Other than courage, their state was bewilderment –
but beyond any need of dignity or respect.
And in case of doubt, their women stayed home,
hampered by equations and prodigious offspring.
All I could see here were desperate men –
twitching to say something righteous or damning.
While others whispered to alert the media,
and haggle for the holy-power of gold.

We remained silent though, and almost composed;
it was a silence that lasted a pompous hour.
Then a rabbi sneezed and the obelisk went down,
resting on its back, but still in the spotlight.
It was shining with its undisturbed anthracite black,
looking very much like a double-blank domino.

I had a choice to make then and I held the faith,
where the scientists seemed only unimpressed.
The holy men demanded at least one miracle,
but finding none forthcoming they left.

Their garments flapping in God's real wind
as they began to walk their angels home.

The scientists left shortly after –
not wishing to be seen in agreement with clerics.
They left with a pretence of professional dismay,
though a mood they had no experimentation to define.
Except in their expressions,
which seemed painfully divine –
and as empty as a moment of rescinded funding.

I knocked on the table then, for want of attention –
an unintended response of sheer frustration.
My honest bones were searching for that something –
for any clue, or moment of revelation –
perhaps a singularity – an acorn – a divination?
An infinite concept that might enlighten a mind.

And then, by luck, in my need to prevail,

I had inadvertently signalled the end of my turn.
The knocking was interpreted in the universal code
as an admission that I could not proceed.

2

The game was afoot though, and I was Sherlock Holmes –
thrown back to the adventure of the windswept beach.
This time, with a deerstalker-hat I found washed up –
perfect for controlling a serious search.
Though to some, it was the symptomatic dress
of an egotistical hero – once more on the loose,
and fallen vagrant.

For nine years of nights and days – then thrice,
I patrolled those sands of ranging wind,
eventually finding the missing dominos –
the twenty-seven slabs of alien code?
But they did seem perfectly good dominos to me –
mysteriously unweathered by sand and sea.
Yet no other miracle had revealed of itself.

After an heroic journey, I returned to my table,
where the double-blank obelisk waited in moonlight.
The lamps were now black as an unpaid bill,

so I lit some candles and began to play on –
adding millions of dominoes, one by one –
until the deed had spread its rhythm, planets wide,
into a precise interlude of ritual knocking…

The Messiah appeared in my living room then,
in the form of a star-child in a glowing sphere.
And Jupiter collapsed into a dwarf star –
becoming a second sun – not far from here.